TRADITIONS AND CELEBRATIONS

HOLI

by Ranjeeta Ramkumar

PEBBLE
a capstone imprint

Published by Pebble, an imprint of Capstone
1710 Roe Crest Drive, North Mankato, Minnesota 56003
capstonepub.com

Copyright © 2024 by Capstone. All rights reserved. No part of this publication may be reproduced in whole or in part, or stored in a retrieval system, or transmitted in any form or by any means, electronic, mechanical, photocopying, recording, or otherwise, without written permission of the publisher.

Library of Congress Cataloging-in-Publication Data is available on the Library of Congress website.

ISBN: 9780756576936 (hardcover)
ISBN: 9780756577179 (paperback)
ISBN: 9780756577186 (ebook PDF)

Summary: Holi is a Hindu festival that celebrates a triumph of good over evil. It is also a celebration of love. People have a bonfire to represent the story of Prahlad and Holika. They gather in the streets to throw colored paint on one another and have a big feast. Discover how people in different places celebrate the festival.

Editorial Credits
Editor: Ericka Smith; Designer: Kayla Rossow; Media Researcher: Svetlana Zhurkin; Production Specialist: Katy LaVigne

Image Credits
Alamy: Dinodia Photos, 13, Maidun Collection, 7, Tim Graham, 27; Getty Images: CR Shelare, 5, Paul Liebhardt, 8, prabhjits, 21, Rangeecha, 1, Tanusree Mitra, 20; Shutterstock: Anil Khadka, 16, B Creativezz, 11, betto rodrigues, 17, CRS Photo, 23, gnanistock, 22, Matjoe, 24, nelle hembry, 29, Rafal Kulik (background), back cover and throughout, Rafinaded, cover, Ramniklal Modi, 19, Rudra Narayan Mitra, 15, Saurav Kumar Boruah, 25

All internet sites appearing in back matter were available and accurate when this book was sent to press.

TABLE OF CONTENTS

WHAT IS HOLI?..4

WHEN IS HOLI?...14

WHO CELEBRATES HOLI? 16

HOW IS HOLI CELEBRATED?.................... 18

GLOSSARY..30

READ MORE...................................... 31

INTERNET SITES 31

INDEX 32

ABOUT THE AUTHOR 32

Words in **bold** are in the glossary.

WHAT IS HOLI?

A multicolored sky. Music and dance. Sweets and feasts. That is what Holi is all about.

Holi is one of the most popular festivals in India. It is a Hindu festival. It celebrates a victory of good over evil.

Holi is known as the "festival of colors." During the festival, people apply colored powders on one another as a celebration of joy and love.

A Holi celebration in India

THE LEGEND BEHIND HOLI

The word *Holi* comes from the name *Holika*. Holika was the sister of the demon King Hiranyakashipu. The king believed he was god. He forced the people in his kingdom to worship him.

King Hiranyakashipu's son Prahlad was a **devotee** of **Lord Vishnu**. Prahlad refused to accept his father as god. That made Hiranyakashipu angry. He asked Holika to help him get rid of Prahlad.

King Hiranyakashipu and Prahlad

Holika and Prahlad

Holika tricked Prahlad into sitting with her in a burning **pyre**. She had special powers that would protect her from the flames. Prahlad prayed to Lord Vishnu to protect him from the danger. Lord Vishnu saved him and destroyed Holika. Good won over evil that day.

THE COLORS OF HOLI

Holi is not just a celebration of good triumphing over evil. It is also a celebration of love. The story of Lord Krishna and Radha might explain why people throw colored powder on one another during Holi.

Lord Krishna was a dark-skinned young boy. He fell in love with a beautiful, light-skinned girl named Radha. But he often complained to his mother about their different **complexions**.

One day his mother suggested that he apply color on Radha's face and change her complexion to any color he wanted. The mischievous boy did just that to Radha and her friends.

This story was passed down through generations. And to this day **smearing** color on others is done as a celebration of the love between Radha and Lord Krishna.

Lord Krishna spraying Radha with paint

WHEN IS HOLI?

On the Hindu calendar, Holi is celebrated on the last full moon day of the month **Phalgun**. It marks the end of winter and the beginning of spring. The festival falls between the months of February and March.

WHO CELEBRATES HOLI?

In the past, Holi was celebrated only by Hindus in northern parts of India and Nepal. Now people of all religions in those countries celebrate the festival. Entire towns come together to celebrate.

A Holi celebration in Nepal

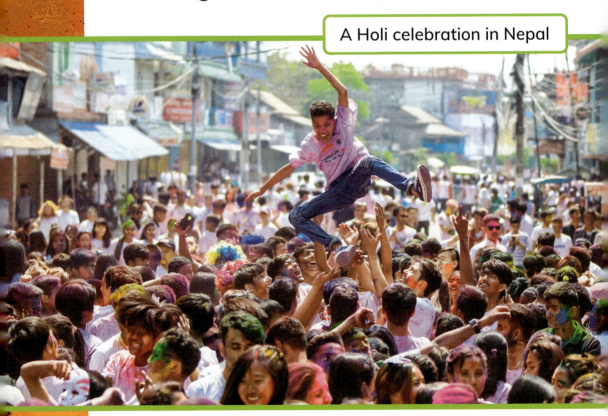

A Holi celebration in the United States

Many Indians live in other countries, so Holi is now a popular international festival. Indian communities all over the world celebrate Holi. Some celebrate with their friends who are not Indian.

HOW IS HOLI CELEBRATED?

Holi is celebrated over two days. The first day is Chhoti Holi—"little Holi." It begins at night. People collect dry leaves and twigs. They build a large bonfire. Then, they burn an **effigy** of Holika, like in the **legend**. People move around the fire and chant holy verses.

The second day is Badi Holi—"great Holi." People gather in large crowds in the streets and throw colored powders or colored water on one another. After the festivities, everyone takes a bath to wash away the colors. This symbolizes cleansing oneself of all evils.

In the evening, they exchange sweets with friends and family. The day ends with a huge feast. Big parties with DJs and musical performances are common in cities.

CELEBRATING HOLI AROUND INDIA

The people of Uttarakhand celebrate a musical Holi. They wear traditional dresses, sing folk songs, and dance. They also go around the village to greet people.

In Vrindavan, Braj, Varanasi, and Nandgaon, people celebrate Lath Mar Holi. In the story of Lord Krishna and Radha, Radha and her friends chase Lord Krishna away with sticks after he smears color on them. So women playfully beat their husbands who use shields to protect themselves.

Holi is called *Shigmo* in Goa. People in Goa celebrate with traditional folk dances, effigies of Holika, parades, and cultural plays. Even tourists take part in the festivities!

People in Assam call Holi *Phakuwa*. On the first day, people burn clay huts to represent the legend of Holika. On the second day, they sing and dance and paint one another with colors.

The royal family of Udaipur in Rajasthan celebrates Holi **grandly**. They have **processions** with decorated horses, elephants, and the royal band.

Later, the family holds a dinner at the royal palace with special guests. The celebration ends with fireworks.

Each state in India has its own Holi customs and traditions. But the excitement and energy of Holi is the same everywhere.

Holi has become so popular that tourists now visit India just for Holi. They want to experience and be a part of one of the most fun festivals in the world!

GLOSSARY

complexion (kuhm-PLEK-shuhn)—the color of a person's skin

devotee (deh-voh-TEE)—follower

effigy (EH-fuh-jee)—a dummy made to look like a hated person

grandly (GRAND-lee)—in a way that's very impressive

legend (LEJ-uhnd)—a story passed down through the years that may not be completely true

Lord Vishnu (LORD VISH-noo)—one of the three supreme gods in Hinduism

Phalgun (fal-GUN)—the twelfth month in the Hindu calendar

procession (pruh-SESH-uhn)—a group of people moving in an orderly way

pyre (PYER)—a pile or heap of burnable materials

smear (SMEER)—to spread something on a person or object

READ MORE

Amin, Anita Nahta. *Diwali.* North Mankato, MN: Capstone, 2022.

Kumari, Priya and Komal Garg. *My Holi: Colors of Cheer.* East Brunswick, NJ: Eternal Tree Books, 2022.

Soundar, Chitra. *Holi Hai!* Chicago: Albert Whitman & Company, 2021.

INTERNET SITES

Britannica Kids: Hinduism
kids.britannica.com/kids/article/Hinduism/353249

Kiddle: Holi Facts for Kids
kids.kiddle.co/Holi

National Geographic Kids: Holi: Festival of Colors
kids.nationalgeographic.com/pages/article/holi

INDEX

Assam, 25
Badi Holi, 20–21
Braj, 23
Chhoti Holi, 18–19
Goa, 24
Holika, 6–9, 18, 24, 25
King Hiranyakashipu, 6–7
Lath Mar Holi, 23
Lord Krishna, 10–13, 23
Lord Vishnu, 6, 9
Nandgaon, 23
Nepal, 16

Phakuwa, 25
Phalgun, 14
Prahlad, 6–9
Radha, 10–13, 23
Rajasthan, 26
royal family, 26
Shigmo, 24
Udaipur, 26
United States, 17
Uttarakhand, 22
Varanasi, 23
Vrindavan, 23

ABOUT THE AUTHOR

Ranjeeta Ramkumar lives in Dubai with her husband, two kids, and two cats. Ranjeeta has worked as a copywriter, scriptwriter, and freelance children's short story writer in the past. Now through her books she tries to spread hope and positivity in kids the world over.